Exploring Stratford-upon-Avon

A guided tour

by
Enid Colston

Meridian Books

Published 1991 by Meridian Books
© Enid Colston 1991

British Library Cataloguing in Publication Data
Colston, Enid
Exploring Stratford-Upon-Avon : a guided tour
  1. Warwickshire. Stratford-Upon-Avon — Visitors guides
  I. Title
  914.2489

  ISBN 1-869922-10-7

Publishers' Note
Every care has been taken in the preparation of this book but the publishers cannot accept responsibilty for any inaccuracies or for any loss, damage or inconvenience resulting from the use of the book.

Meridian Books
40 Hadzor Road
Oldbury
Warley
West Midlands
B68 9LA

Printed by Aston University.

INTRODUCTION

Since my first visit to Stratford upon Avon in 1950 the town has had a fascination for me. Situated as it is on the edge of the West Midlands conurbation it has, despite this, managed to retain much of its rural charm. With its ancient streets and its river running through there is a sense that, despite its expansion in recent times, here is a Stratford upon Avon that Shakespeare, born and brought up in the town, would probably still recognise.

People from all over the world come here to see Shakespeare's plays performed and indeed part of my own pleasure, while compiling this guide, has been recalling past productions at the Shakespeare Memorial Theatre as well as seeing present ones.

In this book I take you on a guided tour of Stratford upon Avon, attempting to show you not only how much of its past can be discovered in its streets and buildings but what there is of more recent origin, too. The main walk is approximately three miles in all. The amount of time taken to complete it depends on how long you allow for studying the features highlighted in the guide; it is easy to spend a half a day looking at the exteriors of buildings alone. If you want to go into the gardens, museums, churches and other buildings and attractions I have noted, you could easily spend a day or more.

It is possible to extend the tour by a mile by walking along the east bank of the river. Directions for this are given on page 21 as are those to Anne Hathaway's Cottage (p. 40) and Mary Arden's House (p. 46), two properties owned by the Shakespeare Birthplace Trust which lie just outside Stratford.

The walk begins and ends at the corner of Bridge Street and Waterside. However, as it is a circular walk you do not necessarily need to start there but can join wherever is most convenient. The increasing pedestrianisation of some of Stratford's streets serves to make the walk more pleasant.

The location of features picked out in capitals — for example, GUILD CHAPEL **(21)** - can be found by referring to the numbers on the map on the following page.

While every care has been taken in compiling information it cannot be guaranteed, in a time of rapid change, that the features described will remain the same. I hope, however, this book will give both visitors and residents alike as much enjoyment as I have had from researching it.

Enid Colston   December 1990.

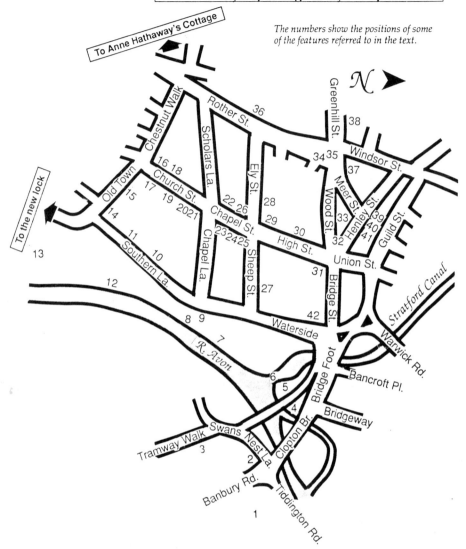

The Route of Exploring Stratford-upon-Avon

To Anne Hathaway's Cottage

The numbers show the positions of some of the features referred to in the text.

ACKNOWLEDGEMENTS

During the research for the book I talked to many people and I am extremely grateful for the patience and understanding that has been afforded to me. I should also like to acknowledge the invaluable additional information that I have obtained through brochures and guide books.

I should particularly like to thank Mr Stan Oldfield who so generously gave of his time to take the photographs.

Exploring
Stratford-upon-Avon

WE START OUR WALK on the busy corner of Bridge Street and Waterside within sight of the River Avon. It was this river that probably first attracted settlers to the area centuries ago, possibly because of the ford that made the river passable here — a ford which in addition, gives the town its name — "straet" a road or street that crosses the ford, thus Stratford.

Diagonally across the road on the left lies the coach and car park from where, throughout the season, an open double-decker bus takes tourists to historic buildings in and around Stratford. Beyond this you can see the modern lines of the Moat House International Hotel and, behind, the Stratford-upon-Avon Sports Centre.

We shall come back to Bridge Street and Waterside later but, now, we must negotiate the traffic and walk over to the left hand side of Bridgefoot, carefully crossing the A34. Keep to that side of the road and continue forward towards the river.

The first narrow stretch of water you meet is the Stratford-upon-Avon Canal which winds its way sluggishly under a small bridge to join the River Avon. Its present relatively deserted air does nothing to remind us how important it was during the first half of the eighteenth century. Stratford, always a prosperous market town, had, at this time, been suffering from a depression. But the building and completion of the canal in 1816 served to stimulate the trade of the town. Grain and flour were sent by canal to Birmingham, coal came from Staffordshire, the stone quarries at Wilmcote were worked as never before. Wharfs were built along Bancroft (the site of the present Bancroft Gardens) which became a canal basin. The river, too, was used for the transportation of merchandise. According to West's *Warwickshire Directory*, issued in 1830, the river at Stratford had been cleared, "wharfs laid out, warehouses upon a most extensive scale erected and railroads laid down by the finest engineers in the kingdom".

However, the canal era was short-lived. With the increased use of railways, the Avon navigation declined. River and canal traffic virtually ceased about 1875. Today, in contrast, instead of loaded barges, you might see a brightly decorated narrowboat with her owner or holiday-makers aboard motoring under the bridge beneath you. After

5

many years of neglect, the navigation of the canal was restored during the years 1961-64. We shall be able to read the plaque marking this event when we return from our visit to the other side of the river.

Continue along Bridgefoot to Clopton Bridge to cross the River Avon to its eastern bank. Clopton Bridge carries the main A34 road from Birmingham to Oxford. The present bridge has been standing here since the end of the fifteenth century. It replaced previous inadequate wooden structures and has proved to be a fine and lasting monument to its builder Sir Hugh Clopton, after whom the bridge is named.

Clopton Bridge

Sir Hugh was a native of Stratford who, after leaving home, became first of all a highly successful merchant and then, in 1492, Lord Mayor of London. He did not forget his birthplace, however, for beside being responsible for the building of the bridge he was a generous benefactor to various institutions in the town. You have to walk along the more recently added footpath at the side of the bridge in order to avoid the continuous stream of cars and heavy lorries rumbling by. It is difficult to believe that "this great and sumptuose" stone bridge with its "14 fine archis", as John Leland described it when he saw it in 1530, could withstand the weight of so much modern traffic. However, at the time of writing the new Stratford Relief Road is near completion crossing the Avon by the old railway bridge further down the river.

6

The little tower you see standing in the middle of the road was a toll-house, built in 1814, a reminder of earlier times when travellers paid directly for the upkeep of the bridge.

Facing us at the southern end of Clopton Bridge is the ALVESTON MANOR HOTEL (1). The site has a fascinating history. Remains of Saxon burials have been found nearby and during mediaeval times monks from Worcester built

The old toll-house

here. You can see the story of their house depicted in stained glass, fashioned by Donald Broke, in the hotel's Cedar Room.

The Alveston Manor has had a variety of owners. One of the most colourful was a Mr Bird who, after the second world war, moved in and refashioned the facade using the wood from scrapped Birmingham trams as window frames and timbers from tank transporters as exterior beams. Despite these vicissitudes, the manor still exhibits Queen Anne windows and a William and Mary gable, while the central portion of the house is Elizabethan. The pretty brick summer house by the bridge is early eighteenth century. This was once in the grounds of the Alveston Manor until major highway alterations left it marooned in the middle of the road on a traffic island.

In the garden of the Alveston Manor there is a magnificent cedar tree which some say served as the setting for the first performance of Shakespeare's *A Midsummer Night's Dream*. Others would dispute this. Nevertheless it has meant that, in modern times, the play has periodically been produced under this tree. On the front lawn stands a statue

Summer House, once in the gardens of Alveston Manor Hotel

of Shakespeare. This was found in the back garden of a house in Leamington Spa and erected here.

You now cross the road to the SWAN'S NEST HOTEL **(2)** situated at the end of Swan's Nest Lane. The Swan's Nest dates from the late seventeenth century and is of special interest because it was one of the earliest houses in Stratford to be built in brick. It shares this distinction with No.5 Chapel Street. The inn started life as The Bear in 1662, shortly before the construction of the present building. In 1673 it was enlarged by Sir John Clopton, on whose land it stood, as part of a scheme for developing the navigation of the river. At one period of its life it was used as a warehouse but was later reopened as the Shoulder of Mutton; the name Swan's Nest is comparatively modern. It is now a listed building.

Now continue along Swan's Nest Lane to reach Tramway Walk which, on the left, is a wide raised track disappearing ahead of you into the trees. On it once lay the tracks of the horse-propelled railway, or "tramway" as it came to be called, designed to link the canal and Avon navigation at Stratford with Shipston-on-Stour and Moreton-in-Marsh. The brick Tramway Bridge, over the river, was built in 1823; the Moreton line was opened in 1826 and the Shipston branch ten years later. On the Stratford - Shipston road is the Old Tramway Inn where the horses were stabled. Its sign depicts the departure from Stratford of a horse team.

If you turn left into Tramway Walk you will encounter a much more recent addition to Stratford — the STRATFORD-UPON-AVON BUTTERFLY FARM AND JUNGLE SAFARI **(3)**. Here 1,000 free-flying tropical and European butterflies, as well as birds, can be seen enjoying the carefully controlled, heated atmosphere suited to their needs. What is claimed as the world's largest species of spiders is housed in Insect City while there is a variety of insect displays. The Butterfly Farm is open all the year round.

Return to Swans Nest Lane and cross this to the section of Tramway Walk opposite. This leads to the Tramway Bridge, now a footbridge, which takes us back across the river. If you look to the right here you have a good view of the fourteen arches of Clopton Bridge.

Just beyond the north end of the Tramway Bridge stands one of the original TRAMWAY WAGONS (4), preserved on a length of track. A memorial here commemorates the engineer William James of Henley-in-Arden who projected, surveyed and largely financed the whole venture which he saw as natural extension to the Stratford Canal for which he was also responsible. The memorial describes how the tramway remained in use until the end of the last century. The track was not taken up, however, until the period of the first World War.

The Tramway Walk

To the left lie the Bancroft Gardens. They are a pleasant place in which to wander, especially on a summer's day, and they gain character from the canal which passes through them down to the Avon. Prominent in the gardens is Lord Ronald Gower's imposing SHAKESPEARE MONUMENT (5). The central stone plinth shows the seated figure of Shakespeare surrounded by Prince Hal with the crown, Hamlet holding Yorick's skull, Lady Macbeth sleep-walking and Falstaff — a reminder that Shakespeare was, in his plays, a master of history, philosophy, tragedy and comedy. The bronze figures were cast in Paris in 1888. The stone used in the monument is partly Boxground Bath, partly York. Originally it stood behind the Memorial Theatre and the unveiling ceremony

9

included speeches by Oscar Wilde. It was moved to its present site in 1933.

The canal is linked to the river by a LOCK **(6)**. Cross this by the bridge, noting as you do a plaque which marks the opening of the completed restoration to navigation of the canal by Queen Elizabeth, the Queen

William Shakespeare

It is perhaps a little disappointing that we don't know more about the life of William Shakespeare, a man whose position in world literature remains supreme. Such facts as there are have to be gleaned from documents of an official character though there are a number of contemporary allusions to him as a writer. The parish register of Holy Trinity Church shows that he was baptised there on 26th April 1564. His birthday is traditionally celebrated on the 23rd April, the same date on which he died.

His father, John Shakespeare, was a burgess of the borough who in 1565 became an alderman and then, in 1568, bailiff(mayor) of Stratford. William's mother, Mary, came from the prosperous Arden family of Wilmcote. With such a background it seems very likely that their son would have gone to the local grammar school. There he would have studied mainly Latin — both language and literature — and might have been expected to have gone to university. Instead he married at the age of eighteen. When and where aren't known. The episcopal registry at Worcester, however, records a bond dated 28th November 1582 executed by two Stratford yeomen as a security to the bishop for the issue of a licence for the marriage of William Shakespeare and Anne Hathaway of Shottery. Their first child, a daughter Susanna, must have been born a few months afterwards as the records of Holy Trinity show that she was baptised 26th May 1583. Her brother and sister, the twins Judith and Hamnet were baptised 2nd February 1585. Hamnet was to die eleven years later.

Then there is a silence for eight years until Shakespeare's name starts appearing in London's theatre world. It isn't clear how his stage career began but from 1594 he was an important member of the Lord Chamberlain's Company of players — called, after the accession of James 1st in 1603, the King's Men. At the Globe Theatre his colleague was the famous actor of the time, Richard Burbage. Shakespeare was certainly prosperous enough to purchase New Place in 1597 and to this, one of the biggest houses in his native town, he retired in 1610. For twenty years he had applied himself successfully to his art of actor and playwright. He died on 23rd April 1616, at the age of fifty-two and was buried in the chancel of the parish church. To his fellow actors, Heminge and Condell, who collected Shakespeare's plays for the first Folio edition, he was "a worthy friend". They and Burbage were remembered in his will. To Ben Jonson, a fellow playwright, he was "not of an age but for all time".

The Shakespeare Monument in the Bancroft Gardens

11

Mother, in 1964. Originally owned by the National Trust, the canal is now under the care of British Waterways. When the weather is fine it is difficult to imagine that there have been occasions when the Avon has burst its banks and flooded the surrounding low-lying land. A line on one of the Waterside cottages, over the road, records a particularly high level of water in 1901.

Now walk forward to the ROYAL SHAKESPEARE THEATRE **(7)** (previously the Shakespeare Memorial Theatre) sited prominently at the further end of the Bancroft Gardens. It is the second theatre to be built here by the river and, like its predecessor, is regarded as the centre of Shakespearian performance. The first theatre, opened in 1879, owed its inception to the vision and enthusiasm of local brewer Charles Edward Flower who not only raised money for the project but also generously donated the land on which the theatre stands. When, in 1926, the theatre was almost completely destroyed by fire a world-wide campaign was launched to provide a new one. The present brick building, designed by Elizabeth Scott, was opened by the Prince of Wales on 23rd April, 1932, the anniversary of Shakespeare's birth. Many eminent actors, actresses and producers have been associated with the theatre as members of the Royal Shakespeare Company, a company whose productions attract an international audience and enjoy an enviable reputation. To emerge from the theatre after a stimulating performance, to see the coloured lights in the trees in the gardens and to look at the river bathed in the shadowy light from the theatre terraces is a memorable experience.

Now take the path on the left of the theatre which overlooks the river. At the back of the theatre you will meet the SWAN THEATRE **(8)** built in 1986 in the burnt out shell of the old Victorian Gothic Shakespeare Memorial Theatre. This has considerably expanded the facilities of the Company. The ambitious scheme of providing a theatre with a promontory stage, especially adapted to the performance of Shakespeare and his more neglected contemporaries, was made possible by a munificent gift from an American benefactor, Frederick R Koch. There is a plaque commemorating his gift in the auditorium of the Swan Theatre.

A striking feature of the Swan Theatre is its soaring roof topped by twin weather vanes. You will get a good view of these by looking back from the Theatre Garden which lies just ahead.

But, first of all, come back to Waterside to visit the LIBRARY AND ART GALLERY **(9)** which was part of the whole Victorian Gothic complex of buildings conceived by Charles Edward Flower when the Shakespeare Memorial Theatre was originally built. The library and gallery, completed in 1881, were the only buildings to survive the fire of 1926.

They were separated from the original theatre by a bridge which is still there today and forms part of the Swan Theatre development.

Exhibitions, associated with the season's plays, are regularly held in the foyer and there is a shop selling books associated with the theatre and its productions. It is possible here to book a backstage tour of both the Swan and the main theatre.

The Royal Shakespeare Theatre

The Art Gallery houses the Royal Shakespeare Theatre collection, representing the art of four centuries, inspired by the texts and performances of Shakespeare's plays. The works range from a seventeenth century wood panel portrait of William Shakespeare to the satirical graphics of twentieth century cartoonist Ronald Steadman. A notable portrait is that of Laurence Olivier as Macbeth by Ruskin Spear R.A.

Temporary exhibitions are mounted using models of stage sets, costume designs, costumes, properties, prompt books, stage plans and production photographs held in the Royal Shakespeare Theatre archives. A charge is made to visit the gallery which is open throughout the year.

As you leave the Library and Art Gallery look up to your right where you will see a lively terra-cotta frieze depicting three scenes from Shakespeare's plays.

Also, look opposite over the road where the lecture hall built in 1887 stands — another part of Charles Flower's scheme to extend the variety of theatrical activities available to his contemporaries. Over the door you will see the inscription "CEF 1887". The building is now used as a workshop for the theatre. Unfortunately the drama school also planned by Charles Flower was never built.

Now walk forward through the theatre garden and alongside the river towards Holy Trinity Church, the tower and spire of which you can see rising majestically above the trees — a famous prospect. On your left, during the summer, a ferry carries foot passengers across the river. There are self-hire boats too. Others can be obtained further upstream just outside the main theatre. To your right, on the other side of the road, is what is possibly Stratford's best known pub, THE BLACK SWAN/DIRTY DUCK **(10)** — the two birds appearing on opposite sides of the inn sign! It is a popular haunt both for visitors and actors from the nearby theatre. Further along, where Waterside becomes Southern Lane, THE OTHER PLACE **(11)**, which has been the home of the Royal Shakespeare Company's experimental productions as well as Shakespeare and the classics, is being rebuilt with a schedule which aims for completion in 1991.

At the end of the Theatre Gardens, on your right, the traditional game of *Nine Men's Morris* has been laid out in the grass, a reminder of Titania's observation in *A Midsummer's Night Dream* — "The nine men's morris is filled up with mud" (Act 2, Sc.1).

We now go through from Theatre Gardens to the Royal Shakespeare Company's Centenary Garden, Avonbank, which was formally opened

Nine Men's Morris

Nine Men's Morris, also called Mill or The Mill, is a board game of some antiquity, most popular in Europe during the fourteenth century, but played throughout the world in various forms. The board is made up of three concentric squares and a number of transverse lines making in all twenty four points of intersection. At these intersections black spots are put to indicate where the pieces or men should be laid. The game is played by two persons with nine pieces each, hence the name nine men's morris. The pieces are placed, alternately, by each player, on the spots. Each endeavours to prevent his opponent from placing three pieces in a row (a mill) without the intervention of a piece belonging to the other. Should either succeed in doing so, he can remove one of his opponents pieces. The player who removes all of his opponent's pieces wins the game. Sometimes when a board wasn't available the figures were drawn on the ground, with holes for the spots.

Library and Art Gallery

by the Queen in 1975. The centenary was not, as might be supposed, of the opening of the Shakespeare Theatre which was 1879, but of the inauguration of the committee which was set up to consider the building of the theatre.

The one remaining building that you see in the garden is the summer house which once belonged to the home, now demolished, of a member of the Flower family. This is now the STRATFORD BRASS RUBBING CENTRE **(12)** where you can make your own brass rubbings from replicas of church brasses. During the season the centre is open daily.

You now have to leave the gardens by going across right towards the road to reach HOLY TRINITY CHURCH **(13)** the spire of which we saw earlier. The street leading to it, and the area in which Holy Trinity lies, is called Old Town; so the original Stratford was probably here, before it developed west of the bridge along the main road. Certainly the name Old Town was known in the thirteenth century.

Holy Trinity is an imposing mediaeval church overlooking the river with its tower, transepts and parts of the nave dating back to the early years of the thirteenth century. The church was enlarged at the beginning

15

The Swan Theatre

of the fourteenth century by John de Stratford, Bishop of Worcester, who added the present north and south aisles. It was this John whose foundation of a chantry in 1331 in a south-aisle chapel dedicated to Thomas à Becket led to the churches confirmation as a college. Though the collegiate role was swept away at the Reformation it is believed that the building in which the priests of the college lived and worked remained until it was demolished at the end of the eighteenth century. Only the name College Street is left as a reminder of its former existence in Old Town.

You approach the entrance to the church through the churchyard by a leafy avenue of lime trees, twelve on the left and eleven on the right. Those on the left represent the twelve tribes of Israel; those on the right

Holy Trinity Church

the twelve apostles but with one, Judas Iscariot, turned traitor, missing. Lying behind the gap is the tree which stands for St. Mathias who took Judas's place. The names cut in the flagstones along the avenue mark family burial vaults — the last burial occurred at the turn of the century.

On the fifteenth century inner door note the thirteenth century sanctuary knocker. In times past any criminal reaching it could claim protection for thirty-seven days.

Sanctuary Knocker on the door of Holy Trinity Church

It is hardly surprising that there are numerous visitors to the church for it is here that Shakespeare was baptised, married and buried. But, as well as containing Shakespeare's tomb and monument, Holy Trinity, with its satisfying interior proportions, has many other interesting features. For instance

Misericords in Holy Trinity Church   Birmingham City Library

18

Hugh Clopton, builder of the bridge, though buried in London, is commemorated in the north aisle by a colourful altar tomb the canopy of which carries the arms of Clopton, The Wool Staplers' Company and the City of London. The effigy of his nephew William with that of William's wife Agnes beside him lie here too on a late Elizabethan tomb-chest while their seven children stand ranged above them on the left against the North wall. In St. Peter's Chapel is the American window — *The Adoration of the Magi* — unveiled in 1896 by the American Ambassador, a gift from the people of the United States of America.

To visit Shakespeare's tomb entails paying a contribution to the restoration fund, at the chancel arch. The chancel was built by Dean Balsall who died in 1491 and whose tomb-chest is situated there. As you walk through the choir stalls note the twenty six finely carved misericords — these are the brackets on the undersides of the hinged choir stall seats which allow the infirm some support when standing. They recall, often in an entertaining way, aspects of life in the fifteenth. century.

Shakespeare's gravestone, marking the place where the poet was buried, lies beyond the altar rails and bears the well-known lines cursing would-be desecrators of his grave:

Good frend for Jesus sake forbeare
To digg the dust encloased heare;
Blest be the man who spare thes stones
And curst be he who moves my bones.

Nearby are the tombs of his wife, Anne Hathaway, his elder daughter, Susanna Hall, and his son-in-law Dr. John Hall. From the chancel wall a near contemporary bust of Shakespeare by Gerard Johnson looks down at us from between two alabaster Corinthian columns — an accurate portraiture? We don't know.

You leave the church through the North door by which you entered, turn right into Old Town and make your way past three characteristic SIXTEENTH CENTURY COTTAGES **(14)**, The Dower House, Avon Croft and

The Shakespeare 'Curse' Birmingham City Library

Old Town Croft. Next is HALL'S CROFT **(15)**, sixteenth century like its neighbours and timber-framed: it is regarded by some as the most rewarding of the Birthplace Trust's Stratford Houses. Purchased by the Shakespeare Birthplace Trustees in 1949 it has been carefully restored to the condition in which it is today.

Shakespeare bust in
Holy Trinity Church

Birmingham City Library

It belonged to Dr. John Hall, a physician renowned in the Midlands, who married Shakespeare's daughter Susanna in 1607 and brought her to live there. Their only daughter Elizabeth was born there the following year. The Halls resided at Hall's Croft until after Shakespeare's death in 1616 when the family moved to New Place.

Dr. Hall's *Select Observations on English Bodies*, a collection of successfully treated cases published after his death, is among exhibits on view in the house illustrating the theory and practice of medicine in Dr. Hall's time. His dispensary is arranged with the jars and manuals of a Jacobean surgery and the rooms are furnished in the style appropriate to a late sixteenth century middle-class home. The walled garden is a delight, secluded and peaceful in the midst of Stratford's hustle and bustle.

Certain rooms in Hall's Croft have been set aside for use as a Festival Club. This is a social and cultural centre with membership open to visitors to Stratford-upon-Avon and to residents. The house is open all the year round to the general public.

The Stratford New Lock

In 1971 the Stratford New Lock was built by men from Gloucester Gaol and other volunteers in order to restore navigation to the Upper Avon. The lock can be reached by taking Mill Lane at the side of Holy Trinity Church down to the river. Cross the river by the footbridge. On your right is the new Stratford relief road. After crossing the Avon turn left onto the path which runs through the recreation ground by the side of the river. It isn't far to the lock which is approached through a small gate. A plaque commemorates the work of the prisoners while, at the same time, dedicating the lock to the memory of Lt. Colonel Sir Fordham Flower who was Chairman of the Upper Avon Navigation Trust. Another plaque tells how, in 1986, improvement of the lock "was greatly assisted by the family of Colin Preston Witter of Chester who was much interested in the restoration of Inland Waterways" and it is his name on the lock which can be seen from the river.

The new lock linking the Stratford canal to the Avon

In 1974 The New Upper Navigation Trust was declared open by Queen Elizabeth, the Queen Mother. To mark the occasion a striking monument, designed by David Hutchings, was erected by the side of the lock. It consists of steel piles similiar to those for building locks and it symbolises the five years, 1969-1974, it took to restore the navigation of the river and the movement of boats.

It is a pleasant walk back to the town of Stratford forward along the side of the river to the Tramway Bridge or you can return the way you came.

Continue past Hall's Croft and turn right into Church Street. This street, like Waterside and Southern Lane, lies parallel to the Avon and forms part of the original mediaeval grid layout of Stratford-upon-Avon bounded by the river to the south-east and Rother Street to the north — a simple and convenient town plan to which it has not been necessary to make any major change over a period of seven hundred years.

Cottages in Old Town

Several buildings catch the eye. On the left TRINITY COLLEGE SCHOOL **(16)** founded in 1870 has been converted into flats. On the right the WINDMILL INN **(17)**, with its squat timber-framed exterior, announces that it has welcomed customers for three hundred and fifty years. It has the oldest unbroken licence in the town.

Almost opposite is MASON CROFT **(18)** where Marie Corelli, the novelist, lived from 1901 until her death in 1924. She was a popular writer of her day who achieved some notoriety in Stratford by her unusual life style. Among her fancies were the Shetland ponies Puck and Ariel which pulled her carriage, and another the gondola in which she was transported about the Avon by an Italian gondolier, Giovanni. Since 1951, however, Mason Croft has been the home of the Shakespeare Institute of the University of Birmingham. This was founded with the intention of promoting international collaboration in Shakespearian scholarship and teaching. The Institute not only encourages research but also provides higher-degree courses, convenes conferences and

22

Hall's Croft

The Windmill Inn

23

organises a large variety of special courses for groups and individuals from all parts of the world. Details of these are available at Mason Croft. The house is not open to the public however.

Continue forward past the modern Stratford District Council offices. On the right hand side of the road you will see a sturdy row of ALMSHOUSES **(19)**, eleven in all. These are part of a fine group of fifteenth century buildings, substantially unaltered since Shakespeare's time, comprising chapel, Guildhall and school, all erected by the Guild of the Holy Cross. The Guild, originally religious and social in its objectives, had become a powerful influence in the community in mediaeval times. In effect it was the ruling body of Stratford of that period with an extensive and influential membership. Made prosperous by gifts and bequests from its members, it owned a good deal of property in the town, the income of which it used for a variety of projects. The Almshouses were built to provide homes for local aged people and this use has continued down to the present time. The Guild survived the dissolution of religious houses in Henry VIII's reign. It was reported upon by commissioners appointed to survey guilds and colleges in 1546, however, and despite the fact that the townspeople preferred to use the Guild chapel rather than the more distant parish church the Guild came to an end in 1547, shortly after the accession of Edward VI.

A little further on we reach, on the right, the entrance to the GRAMMAR SCHOOL **(20)**, a two-storied timber-framed structure erected in the fifteenth century, originally the Guildhall, which lies behind the almshouses in the right angle formed by Church Street and Chapel Lane. The Guild of the Holy Cross held its meetings and feasts here and also paid a schoolmaster to teach in its school. The ground floor was the Guildhall proper, the overhanging upper floor was called the Over Hall.

From 1553, soon after the suppression of the Guild, the Over Hall (now known as Big School) was used as a schoolroom thus continuing the educational traditions already established there previously by the Guild in another building. Since education at the school was free to the sons of burgesses, Shakespeare would have attended classes here though, unfortunately, no contemporary list of pupils survives. In the lower hall Shakespeare may have watched his first play performed by one of the travelling companies under the protection of great noblemen. Was one of his schoolmasters the model for Holofernes in *Love's Labour's Lost*?

The building is now incorporated into the present King Edward VI school. It is open by special arrangement for organised parties during the Easter and summer holidays on application to the headmaster.

Plaque on Mason Croft

The GUILD CHAPEL **(21)** stands on the corner of Church Street and Chapel Lane. A chapel has been in existence here since the thirteenth century for the Guild's primary object was to ensure that masses were said for the souls of the dead and the Guild maintained priests for this purpose. The present nave, tower and porch were added by Hugh Clopton, the same Clopton who built the bridge and, no doubt, masses were said for the salvation of his soul and those of other members of his family. His arms are sported by an angel in the north doorway, under a porch alongside recently restored gargoyles.

The interior of the chapel is cool and inviting. Over the chancel arch remains of a wall-painting can be seen — *The Day of Judgement*, otherwise known as *The Doom*. Placed in full view of the congregation it would, in mediaeval times, have provided both an encouragement and a warning. To the right of the picture small naked figures (apart from a clearly identifiable pope and bishop!) are welcomed into heaven by St. Peter. On the left devils hurl the damned into the fiery cauldron of hell. Note too the remains of wall-paintings of St Thomas à Becket and St. George at the west end of the chapel. In addition there is an interesting reproduction, made by a previous art master at King Edward VI School, of the mediaeval *Dance of Death* which it is believed was situated along the north wall.

Hugh Clopton is commemorated by a monument erected in 1708.

Leave the Guild Chapel and return to the corner of Church Street. This now becomes Chapel Street with the FALCON HOTEL **(22)** on the left hand

25

Almshouses in Church Street

◀ corner and the site of New Place on the opposite corner. The Falcon Hotel has a striking exterior essentially of c.1500 but with a top storey c.1645. Its name is a reminder of the Falcon in the Shakespeare family crest.

NEW PLACE **(23)**, the house where Shakespeare died on 23 April 1616, was originally built toward the end of the fifteenth century by the same enterprising Hugh Clopton of whom we've heard so much in this walk.

The Guild Chapel

26

Interior of the Guild Chapel

27

Shakespeare bought the half-timbered house with its barns and gardens in 1597 for the sum of £60 although he did not take up permanent residence there with his family until 1610. After his death the house passed to his daughter Susanna who moved there with her husband Dr. John Hall from Hall's Croft. Their position in the town is demonstrated by the fact that Susanna entertained Queen Henrietta Maria, Charles I's queen, for three days at New Place in 1643. Subsequently the house was owned by Elizabeth Hall, the poet's granddaughter but, after her death and that of her second husband, it was sold out of the family. New Place came to an ignominious end in the middle of the eighteenth century when the then owner, the Reverend Francis Gastrell, became, first of all, so irritated by visitors coming to see the mulberry tree said to have been planted by Shakespeare that he had it cut down. And then he was so annoyed with the town authorities over rate assessments that he had the house demolished. Now only the foundations remain. Perhaps this is not too great a loss as much of Shakespeare's "praty house of bricke and tymbre" had already gone in rebuilding. In 1862 the site was purchased

The Falcon Hotel

28

for preservation as a national memorial to the poet and was later vested in the capable hands of the Shakespeare Birthplace Trust.

The approach to the foundations of New Place is through Nash's House (entrance to which a charge is made) which stands alongside the site of New Place. Nash's House was the home of Shakespeare's granddaughter Elizabeth Hall, whose first husband was Thomas Nash. It is pleasant to look through the rooms before going into the ornamental gardens outside. The front exterior is mostly imitation but the interior contains much of the original timberwork. The house is furnished in Tudor and Jacobean style with some particularly fine examples of

Nash's House

29

contemporary domestic furniture — the new framed tables of the time with carved legs and the chairs, some with upholstery.

Nash's House also serves as Stratford's local history museum. It includes exhibits from Saxon and Roman times which illustrate the town's early making. David Garrick's link with Stratford is commemorated here while there are many examples of artefacts connected with the ordinary lives of local inhabitants.

The gardens of New Place can be reached now from Nash's House. They provide a delightful setting at the corner of Chapel Street and Chapel Lane where the foundations of the house can be seen. Forming part of the site is a replica of an Elizabethan knott garden.

A gateway from the knott garden leads on to a terrace with a sun-dial overlooking the Great Garden, once the orchard and kitchen garden belonging to New Place, now an attractive expanse of lawn with trees — including an ancient mulberry tree grown from a cutting of a tree planted by Shakespeare himself — and colourful flower beds. You can go into the Great Garden this way or, alternatively, there is another entrance in Chapel Lane much used throughout the day by residents and visitors alike in order to enjoy a peaceful interlude there. This entrance to the garden was provided by the Trustees of Shakespeare's Birthday Trust as a token of appreciation to Sir Fordham Flower O.B.E., Chairman of the Trust 1946-1966. As you emerge from the gardens you will see, on the opposite side, the modern buildings of King Edward VI School while to the left down Chapel Lane there is a view of the Royal Shakespeare Theatre.

Return to the corner of Chapel Lane and turn right into Chapel Street. This time continue past the site of New Place and Nash's House. Immediately on your right is the long range of the SHAKESPEARE HOTEL **(24)** which dates back to 1637. Originally three separate buildings, it has had a varied architectural history. At the beginning of the nineteenth century, for instance, the landlord of the time decided to improve the hotel by refronting the structure with Regency stucco and building a handsome portico out on to the street. Later when tastes changed and it was felt that the exposure of the original timbers would be more in keeping with the hotel's name, the rough-cast was removed. The building was further restored in this century when the front wall was rebuilt in Elizabethan style while the portico was taken to Bridge Street to provide an entrance for the Red Horse, once the Shakespeare's greatest rival as a coaching inn. The Red Horse no longer exists — it is now a Marks and Spencer store — but the portico can still be seen there.

It was at the Red Horse that Washington Irving wrote his account of Stratford in his *Sketch Book* and the hotel was always an attraction to American visitors.

If you look back from the Shakespeare Hotel you have a view of the Almshouses curving away in the distance. Looking forward, at the corner of Chapel Street and Sheep Street, stands the TOWN HALL **(25)**. This civilised Palladian building of cream-coloured Cotswold stone was erected in 1767 to replace the old seventeenth century Market Hall which had fallen into a ruinous state.

The Town Hall

The Town Hall is interesting not only in its own right but for its associations with the famous Shakespearian actor David Garrick. As the Town Hall reached completion Garrick was approached by the then Town Clerk to see if he would offer a gift towards the new building. A financial donation was not what was required, rather a tangible object which would reflect the prestige both of Garrick and Stratford-upon-Avon. In return Garrick would become an Honorary Burgess of Stratford while the documents acknowledging this would be presented to him in a mulberry wood box. Garrick accepted the idea with enthusiasm. His gift was the statue of Shakespeare which still adorns the wall of the Town Hall: by John Cheere it is a copy of Scheemaker's statue in Westminster Abbey.

31

The Town Hall was dedicated by David Garrick at the widely-publicised Shakespeare Jubilee Festival in 1769. What was originally meant to be a relatively simple opening ceremony became, under Garrick's auspices, a three day event which took over the town and its inhabitants. A magnificent amphitheatre, lit by a chandelier of eight hundred lights and with seating for a thousand was erected on the Bancroft near the river. It was here, on the second day, that Garrick performed his *Ode upon Dedicating a Building, and Erecting a Statue, to Shakespeare* to the great admiration of the assembled company. It was unfortunate that the wet weather deprived them of an open-air ceremony where they might have seen the statue hoisted into position. Despite the weather, however, which meant the cancellation of several activities, it seems that a thoroughly good time was had by all with music, dancing, fireworks, the firing of cannons and other jollities. Garrick maintained what would now be called a high profile throughout and there is no doubt that his visit gave a real impetus to Stratford's rising popularity as a literary shrine.

Garrick's gift to the town did not end with the statue. He also commissioned portraits of Shakespeare and himself to be hung inside the new building. These portraits — one of Shakespeare seated in his study by Benjamin Wilson and one of Garrick specially painted for the Corporation by Gainsborough at a cost of sixty guineas — remained in the ballroom until 1946 when they were destroyed by a fire which seriously damaged the upper storey of the Town Hall. A descendant of Garrick presented the portrait by Nathaniel Dance *Garrick as Richard III* which hangs there now. A copy of the Gainsborough hangs in the library of nearby Charlecote Park, the home of the Fairfax-Lucy family.

Before leaving Chapel Street take a look at the MIDLAND BANK (26) on the corner of Chapel Street and Ely Street, opposite the Town Hall. Attractively built in red brick and terra-cotta with an angle turret, the bank has a frieze depicting scenes from Shakespeare's plays.

At this point it is convenient to explore Sheep Street which runs down to Waterside and Bancroft Gardens. This is another of Stratford's mediaeval streets though, now, the shop fronts are modern and the restaurants are geared to the needs of the cosmopolitan clientele which Stratford attracts. Turn right into Sheep Street past the Town Hall. As you walk along the right-hand side pause to look through to the yards behind the frontages. Now often filled with tubs of colourful flowers they once gave access to stables and gardens and, in the nineteenth century, to little groups of labourers' cottages built in courts behind the main street frontages. The most notorious example was Emms Court, ten or eleven tiny dwellings squeezed into the site behind No. 12. They have, of course, since been demolished.

At the bottom of Sheep Street turn round and return along the other side of the road to the junction of Chapel Street and High Street. Many of the houses on this side were damaged by fire at the end of the sixteenth century and considerable rebuilding took place. The restored SHRIEVE'S HOUSE **(27)**, now No. 40 Sheep Street, was reconstructed and enlarged at this time. Unlike many of Stratford's half-timbered buildings it has

The Shrieve's House

not been converted to modern shop use and it has retained many of its original features. It possesses, for instance, a particularly fine bay window overlooking the street, and a high gateway leading to original outbuildings at the rear. Alongside Shrieve's House is a new shopping centre called Shrieve's Walk.

No. 42 is another house which would have been home to a wealthy seventeenth century Stratford tradesman and, like its neighbour, has a domestic appearance which other buildings in the street have lost.

At the upper end of Sheep Street, where it joins High Street, there are shops and offices, built in 1963. The statue on the outside is by Frank Kormis.

Cross High Street and go a little way down Ely Street where a passageway on the right leads to the STRATFORD-UPON-AVON ANTIQUES CENTRE **(28)**, open seven days a week from 10.00am. to 5.30pm., a warren of antique dealers' stalls and showrooms selling a variety of antiques, bric-a-brac and curiosities.

After exploring the antique shops retrace your steps and turn left along High Street. The houses here suffered — primarily, it is thought, because of their thatched roofs — the same disastrous fires in 1594 and 1595 as

33

had affected Sheep Street. However whereas, in Sheep Street, few of the houses built at that time remain, High Street still retains many of its fine Tudor buildings. To this period belongs the TUDOR HOUSE **(29)** on the corner of Ely Street and High Street as well as its neighbour the Garrick Inn. Next door is the ornate three-storied building, now known as Harvard House, built in 1596, by Thomas Rogers butcher and alderman of Stratford. You can see the date 1596 carved beneath the window of the first floor. Around the date are the initials WR, TR and AR indicating members of the Rogers' family. Thomas is remembered especially as the grandfather of John Harvard who, born in London and educated at Emmanuel College Cambridge, was instrumental in founding Harvard College. In 1909 the novelist Marie Corelli arranged for the purchase of the house by a wealthy Harvard man, Edward Morris of Chicago, in order to preserve it as a historic landmark. Its interior is as striking as its exterior. Particularly impressive is the front room upstairs with its oak panelling and open fireplace surmounted by a plaster overmantel decorated with a Tudor rose. At the present time the only income

The Garrick Inn (left) and Harvard House (right)

available to the Trustees for maintaining Harvard House comes from the admission fees of visitors. A more secure future for the house is being planned.

More modern is the BELL COURT **(30)** shopping precinct about half-way along High Stret on the left and the adjacent multi-storey car-park abutting onto Rother Street.

Quiney's House

At the end of High Street you will see, on the opposite side, QUINEY'S HOUSE **(31)**, until recently occupied by the Tourist Information Centre. This was once the home of Shakespeare's daughter Judith, whose husband Thomas Quiney set up here as a wine merchant. Older visitors may remember its earlier function as tearooms to which Judith Shakespeare gave her name.

Do not cross the road but turn left from High Street into Wood Street. On the corner of Wood Street and Henley Street observe the elegant white building, now a bank, but once the MARKET HOUSE **(32)** built in the Regency era.

35

Start walking along Wood Street. Worthy of note, on the other side of the road, among less distinguished buildings, are Nos 44-45, sixteenth century again, and alongside, NUMBER 47 **(33)**, a late seventeenth century brick house with a Dutch gable.

Continue forward past the shops until you arrive in Rother Street. Pause for a moment, however, at the corner of Wood Street and Rother Street to look at the timber-framed building on the corner, Nos. 26-28.

The old market house

This dates from the early sixteenth century and records show that it was once tenanted by a woollen draper, William Parsons, who also held the office of bailiff in 1590 and 1611.

The funnel-shaped end of Rother Street forms Stratford's MARKET PLACE **(34)**, a reminder, if one were needed, that for over seven hundred years Stratford-upon-Avon's existence has been founded primarily on its function as a market town and not as a tourist centre. The tourist trade which constitutes a great deal of its life today came much later. By the time of Shakespeare's birth Stratford was prosperous and established. It had been an incorporated borough for eleven years with a bailiff, fourteen aldermen and fourteen capital burgesses. It had been granted a market by King Richard I as early as 1196 and fairs were held at recognised times. One of them, the Stratford Mop, the old hiring fair, still exists today, though no longer, of course, serving its original purpose. It is held annually at the beginning of October.

The open market takes place every Friday in Rother Market and you can still buy local cheeses and vegetables there. The name Rother comes from an Old English word meaning cattle. In fact the present-day cattle market adjoins the railway station on the Alcester Road. Shakespeare used the term in *Timon of Athens* — "it is the pasture lards the rother's sides" and a quotation from the same play appears on the rather unusual memorial standing in the centre of Rother Market. Known as the AMERICAN DRINKING FOUNTAIN **(35)** and designed by Jethro Cousins of Birmingham, it was presented by George W. Childs, a Philadelphia journalist, and unveiled by Henry Irving who drank the first cupful of water. The foundation stone was laid in 1887 as part of the celebrations to mark Queen Victoria's Golden Jubilee. Today taxis circle round its base.

It would be a pity to miss MASON'S COURT **(36)**, a dwelling house of the Tudor period. Turn left down Rother Street and you will find Mason's Court between the police station and the Christadelphian Hall on the west side of the street. Sensitive restoration has ensured that many of its original features remain — its roughly hewn timber framing, the overhanging roof of hand made tiles and the attractive chimney stacks of narrow bricks.

Return now to the Market Place. Overlooking it, opposite the American Drinking Fountain, is another of Stratford's traditional hotels, the WHITE SWAN **(37)**, an imposing half-timbered building some of which dates from the fifteenth century. Though considerably altered in later times, the hotel still retains many features of interest. One of these is the early sixteenth century mural depict-

The American Fountain

ing *Tobias and the Angel* which can be seen in the Oak Room. During the second world war the hotel was used as a Red Cross Centre for American troops — another pleasing connection that Stratford has with America.

To the west of the square at 19 Greenhill Street is the intriguing TEDDY BEAR MUSEUM **(38)**, founded by Gyles and Michele Brandreth. Here is a

37

Mason's Court

The White Swan

The Teddy Bear Museum

collection of teddy bears from around the world including our own Winnie the Pooh, Rupert and Paddington. The museum is open every day.

From here return the few yards back to Market Place, turn left into Windsor Street and then right into the newly-pedestrianised Henley Street. On the left-hand side you will find the SHAKESPEARE CENTRE **(39)** and, next door, Shakespeare's Birthplace.

The Shakespeare Centre, a modern building designed by Laurence Williams, houses the administrative headquarters of the Shakespeare Birthplace Trust, an influential body which has cared for matters Shakespearian in Stratford for over a century.

The Trust came into existence after the purchase of Shakespeare's Birthplace as a national memorial in 1847. It is an independent charity the aims of which are to promote appreciation of William Shakespeare's life and work and to maintain the various properties connected with his life in Stratford. As well as Shakespeare's Birthplace, the Trust owns New Place and Hall's Croft (which we visited earlier) — also Anne Hathaway's Cottage and Mary Arden's House, where Shakespeare's mother lived. The Trust is active in the educational field, arranging

A Walk to Anne Hathaway's Cottage

Anne Hathaway, Shakespeare's wife, came from the pretty hamlet of Shottery which lies one mile west of Stratford-upon-Avon. Though Shottery is now linked with Stratford it still retains much of its old-world charm with its picturesque village green and thatched cottages. If you are energetic enough you can walk from Stratford along field paths that Shakespeare might very well have used in his courting days. Allow about half an hour to get there — perhaps slightly longer if you are walking from the centre of Stratford.

The path proper, signposted to Anne Hathaway's Cottage, leaves Evesham Road at its junction with Grove Road and Rother Street. It passes between the back gardens of a modern housing estate, across

Ann Hathaway's Cottage

40

three roads, then into the recreation ground (Shottery Fields). There, follow the path diagonally across the field. At the other side take the right fork — the Girls' Grammar school will be on your left.

The right fork brings you to Tavern Lane in the small attractive hamlet of Shottery. Continue round the corner to reach the crossroads, just past the Garden Centre. Anne Hathaway's Cottage lies ahead on the left hand side of Cottage Lane. The way is well signposted.

The title **Anne Hathaway's Cottage** would seem to be a misnomer for when you turn down Cottage Lane you see in front of you a substantial timber-framed building, a yeoman's homestead rather than a cottage. This is because originally it was a farmhouse, known as Hewlands, the home of successive generations of the well established and respected Hathaway family. Their occupancy and ownership ceased in 1892 when the house was bought by the Shakespeare Birthplace Trust. A good number of the present furnishings in the Cottage actually belonged to the Hathaways which makes a visit here even more interesting. There is, for instance, the Hathaway bed, a dark oak, finely carved, four-poster. You can see this in the chamber at the top of the stairs. Here, too, you can see the pair of curved oak timbers or "crucks", pegged together at the top, which was one of the earliest constructional methods used in house building in this country.

Downstairs are the hall or living room and the kitchen. Both are fine rooms with large wide open hearths — a feature, as we have noticed elsewhere, of Elizabethan farmhouses. Both have solid stone-flagged floors as has the Buttery which for centuries has served as a dairy and store for farm produce.

To reach the gardens you first pass through a shop in which a variety of gifts can be bought. The garden is a true cottage garden, planted with traditional shrubs, flowers and herbs, the sight and scent of which are a delight, especially in the summer. Adjoining the garden is an orchard with old fruit trees and wild flowers, providing a perfect setting for the house. In their efforts to improve the properties they own, the Trustees of the Shakespeare Birthplace Trust have planted an area of woodland as a long-term forestry project. This lies alongside the car park provided for visitors to the Cottage.

It is possible to take a slightly different route back to Stratford. Instead of returning via Tavern Lane turn right into the village as you leave Cottage Lane. Go past the inn on your left. The Post Office is further on, on your right. As the road bends round to the right take the path on your left back to Shottery Fields. This time take the left-hand path along the edge of the recreation ground, passing *en route* an adventure playground for small children. Where the path joins the road (The Willows) turn left and then immediately right onto the cycle path alongside the College of Further Education. This path crosses the old railway line, now overgrown and disused. If you bear to the left you will then join the main Alcester Road. Here you turn right, keeping straight ahead now to Stratford town centre.

courses, lectures and study facilities for both students and teachers. It has an outstanding library comprising the combined collections of the Trust and the Royal Shakespeare Theatre. Its archival material relating to Stratford-upon-Avon and Warwickshire is rightly famous. The Trust is self-financing, depending almost entirely on admission charges to the Shakespearian properties and the profit on sales to visitors.

The Shakespeare Centre

The first part of the Shakespeare Centre was completed in 1964 to commemorate the four hundredth anniversary of Shakespeare's death. A relief by the entrance, and the statue of Shakespeare inside, are by Douglas Wain Hobson. The figures engraved in the glass doors are the work of John Hutton who also engraved the West Window of Coventry Cathedral. You will also see a handsome plaque outside describing the contributions made by other nations towards the cost. A similar plaque marks the opening of an extension in 1980. It is through this extension that you gain access to SHAKESPEARE'S BIRTHPLACE (40), possibly the most visited of the Shakespearian properties.

Shakespeare's Birthplace, though now detached, was formerly part of a continuous frontage of shops and houses in Henley Street. The buildings, which were once on either side, were demolished in 1857 to lessen the risk of fire for, by then, the property was marked out for preservation as a permanent memorial to Shakespeare. No record of when the house was built survives but its architecture suggests that much of it dates from the late fifteenth or early sixteenth century. Like many houses in Stratford it is built of local materials — timber from the Forest of Arden and stone from the Wilmcote quarries.

John Shakespeare, William's father, was living there in 1552. At that time the property consisted of two buildings, one of which served as the

Shakespeare's birthplace

Shakespeare's family home and the other a shop, used in connection with John's trade as a glover and wool dealer. Tradition has it that the western part of the building was William's birthplace.

After John's death the property stayed in the family, passing successively to William, to his daughter Susanna, and then to his granddaughter Elizabeth. In 1670 she bequeathed it to her cousin Thomas Hart, William's grandnephew. His descendants in turn continued to own the premises until 1806 when they were sold to Thomas Court for £210. Meanwhile, the eastern part, which had been

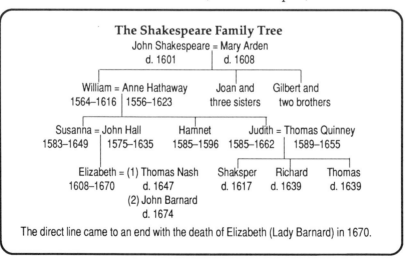

The Shakespeare Family Tree

John Shakespeare = Mary Arden
d. 1601   d. 1608

William = Anne Hathaway   Joan and   Gilbert and
1564–1616   1556–1623   three sisters   two brothers

Susanna = John Hall   Hamnet   Judith = Thomas Quinney
1583–1649   1575–1635   1585–1596   1585–1662   1589–1655

Elizabeth = (1) Thomas Nash   Shaksper   Richard   Thomas
1608–1670   d. 1647   d. 1617   d. 1639   d. 1639
          (2) John Barnard
              d. 1674

The direct line came to an end with the death of Elizabeth (Lady Barnard) in 1670.

Hornby Cottage

John Shakespeare's shop, had, for the previous century, been leased as the Swan and Maidenhead Inn.

Two of the old inn signs have survived, one of them bearing the name of the proprietress, Elizabeth Court, following whose death the property was again offered for sale in 1847. Since then, as we have seen, the property has been administered by a body of Trustees on behalf of the nation. It has been restored to what it looked like on a drawing of 1769.

The layout of the two-storied building is easy to follow; the western portion represents the house where Shakespeare was born and is furnished in period style. The stone-flagged floor of the living-room downstairs is believed to be original as is the wooden staircase leading to the upstairs rooms from the adjoining kitchen. Another doorway from the living room gives access to the museum, originally John Shakespeare's shop. Here there is a variety of exhibits of Shakespearian interest which trace the history and associations of the Birthplace.

44

Upstairs the exhibits relate particularly to Shakespeare. Especially interesting is the old Grammar School desk such as the poet might have used when he was a boy — in fact tradition has it that it is his desk.

You reach the Birthroom, a simple low-pitched chamber over the living-room, from the museum. There is no documentation to confirm its celebrity but, at the same time, there is no reason to doubt that William Shakespeare was very probably born here. Certainly other famous people thought so and, on the window panes, you can see their diamond-scratched signatures to indicate that they had been there. The signatures include those of Sir Walter Scott, Thomas Carlyle, Isaac Watts, Henry Irving and Ellen Terry. Needless to say these were made before the house passed under the control of the Trustees!

The two upstairs rooms at the back of the birthroom were originally bedrooms and from them another staircase now leads down into the garden. This has been as decoratively and thoughtfully laid out as have the other gardens owned by the Birthplace Trust. There are wide borders of herbaceous flowers and specimens of plants and trees which were well known in Shakespeare's day. In the middle of the path at the rear of the house is the base of the mediaeval stone cross which formerly stood at the top of Bridge Street.

From the garden you can return to Henley Street through HORNBY COTTAGE **(41)** which also existed in Shakespeare's time and which now houses a gift shop. It was given to the Birthplace Trust by Andrew Carnegie of New York in 1903.

The Public Library, next door, was also originally a medieval building. By 1901, however, it was in such a bad state of repair that it was scheduled for demolition. It was saved largely through the efforts of Marie Corelli who lobbied energetically for its conservation. Although much of the external timbering is modern, inside it is still possible to see some fine old roof timbers. The foundation of the renovated building was laid on Edward VIII's Coronation Day, 9th August 1902.

Bridge Street, as its name implies, is the street leading to the bridge — the old main street of the town. As you look down towards the river you will see how much wider it is than the other streets. This is because, in times past, it was divided by a row of buildings, called Middle Row, into Fore Bridge Street and Back Bridge Street. Here the principal inns and shops of the town were concentrated as well as the houses of some of the leading tradesmen in the community. Middle Row was itself divided by an alley, providing access from Fore Bridge Street to Back Bridge Street just as now Cook's Alley links Henley Street with Wood Street.

Each year, on or near Shakespeare's birthday, the ceremony of unfurling the flags of the nations takes place in Bridge Street when official representatives of the countries of the world come to Stratford to take part in the traditional birthday celebrations. Carrying colourful posies of flowers and led by civic dignitaries, they process to Holy Trinity Church there to pay homage to the poet and lay flowers on his tomb.

Continue forward along Bridge Street and you are soon at the same busy place at which you started your walk. Just round the corner along Waterside you might just have time to visit THE WORLD OF SHAKESPEARE (42), an "experience in sound and vision" which is shown every hour.

Mary Arden's House

Just over three miles to the north of Stratford-upon-Avon in the village of Wilmcote is **Mary Arden's House**. Acquired by the Shakespeare Birthday Trust in 1930 it originally belonged to Shakespeare's mother's family, the Ardens, who lived there in the sixteenth century. They were leading yeomen of the district. Mary was one of eight daughters of Robert Arden and it was she who in 1557 married John Shakespeare of Snitterfield. Their wedding took place at another nearby local village, Aston Cantlow. Their son, William, was born seven years later. Mary's own father had died in 1556. We are fortunate to have the inventory of Robert Arden's goods, taken after his death, for the items described there — the tables, benches, chests and cupboards, the beds and bedding, the cooking utensils, the wheat and straw in the barns, the ploughs and harrows and livestock — give us some idea of the background of the Arden farmstead and the early years of Shakespeare's mother. It has also helped to provide the basis for the more recent furnishing of this typical Warwickshire farmhouse and its development as a museum of English rural life. The fact that it remained a working farm until 1930 has meant that, despite minor alterations and improvements, the basic structure and layout of the farm premises are very much the same as they were in Shakespeare's day. The yards and barns, too, have kept their original character.

The substantial timber-framing of the house is supported by a solid foundation of Wilmcote stone. The roof, with its attractive dormer windows, is covered with hand-made clay tiles, the colours of which blend sympathetically with the grey stone and bleached oak timbers.

The interior of the building is similarly satifying. Access is through the door at the back which lies at the end of the central passage opposite the front door. Downstairs the kitchen and the dairy are on view as well as the Great Hall and the servants' room. The kitchen, with its pinkish-grey flagged floor, has a large open fireplace where the cooking would have been done. The Great Hall is a bigger room which served as the principal living apartment. Once open to the roof, it was subsequently converted

46

into two storeys by the insertion of a floor supported by a massive beam. Upstairs the bedrooms, with their irregular floors, are simply furnished, serving to emphasise the huge oak timbers used in the construction of the house. Indeed, complete, roughly shaped trees form some of the principal beams.

At the rear of the house the original farmyard has been grassed over but many outbuildings have been preserved intact. Particularly fine is the dovecote which has 657 nesting holes built inside its walls while, at the entrance to the rickyard, is a cider mill. In the high- gabled barns of brick and limestone you can see a comprehensive exhibition of farming implements as well as other reminders of life as it has been lived for generations in the Warwickshire countryside. Notice the staddle stones in the rickyard which kept the hayricks above ground level, free from marauding rats.

Adjoining Mary Arden's House is the Glebe Farm, a collection of farm buildings of similar age which you can reach through a small paddock. Here it has been possible to expand the displays of local farming, craft and rural life material. A smithy has been reconstructed complete with forge, bellows and shoeing tools used by the village blacksmith while the farmhouse has been furnished as it might have been at the beginning of this century. The whole complex is open to the public.

Mary Arden's Cottage

Other Outdoor Guides from Meridian:

Town Guides

WALKABOUT YORK
by Ivan E Broadhead.
Second Edition ISBN 1 869922 08 5   £1.95   48 pages, 51 photographs.

EXPLORING LEEDS
by Ivan E Broadhead
ISBN 0 906070 05 8   £1.95   52 pages, 38 photographs.

EXPLORING HARROGATE
by Ivan E Broadhead
ISBN 0 906070 08 2   £1.95   44 pages, 31 photographs.

EXPLORING KNARESBOROUGH
by Arnold Kellett
ISBN 0 906070 10 4   £1.95   44 pages, 36 photographs.

NORTHAMPTON
by Tony Noble
ISBN 1 869922 06 9   £2.95   64 pages, 34 photographs.

EXPLORING BIRMINGHAM
by Peter Groves
ISBN 1 869922 00 X   £1.95   52 pages, 43 photographs.

Walking Guides

WATERSIDE WALKS in the MIDLANDS
Edited by Peter Groves
ISBN 1 869922 09 3   £3.95   112 pages, 28 photographs, 22 maps.

WATERSIDE WALKS in NORTH YORKSHIRE
by Ivan E Broadhead
ISBN 1 869922 07 7   £3.95   96 pages, 32 photographs, 20 maps.

BEYOND THE BARS
Ten Walks from York City Walls by Ivan E Broadhead
ISBN 1 869922 05 0   £5.95   192 pages, 84 photographs, 10 maps.

LET'S WALK
by Mark Linley
ISBN 1 869922 03 4   £4.95   144 Pages.
Illustrated with 135 sketches and cartoons. *The complete guide to walking in the countryside.*

Touring Guides

EXPLORING NORTHAMPTONSHIRE
by Tony Noble
Second Edition ISBN 1 869922 01 8   £4.95   152 pages, 61 photographs, 24 maps.

Available from booksellers or, if in difficulty, direct from Meridian Books. Please send remittance, adding for postage and packing: order value up to £5.00 add 75p; over £5.00 add £1.00.

MERIDIAN BOOKS, 40 Hadzor Road, Oldbury, Warley, West Midlands, B68 9LA.
Tel: 021-429 4397

Prices subject to possible revision. Please send s.a.e. for our full catalogue.